Gathering Sound

Gathering Sound

Poems by Susan Davis

Winner of the 2005 Rhea & Seymour Gorsline Poetry Competition

FAIRWEATHER BOOKS • BROWNSVILLE, OREGON

First Edition 2 3 4 5 6 7 8 9

Library of Congress Cataloging in Publication Data
Susan Davis,
Gathering Sound
ISBN-10: 0-9771973-4-4
ISBN-13: 978-0-9771973-4-7
Library of Congress Control Number: 2006928242

Fairweather Books is an imprint of
Bedbug Press
P.O. Box 39
Brownsville, OR 97327
www.bedbugpress.com

Cover Photo: John Rosenthal
Author Photo: Michael Czeiszperger
Design: Cheryl McLean

Printed by Thomson-Shore, Inc., Dexter, MI.

This book is printed on acid-free paper.

Acknowledgments

Grateful acknowledgment is made to the editors of the following magazines where some of these poems first appeared (at times in a different form):

The Paris Review: "The Endless Story"
The Boston Review: "Gertrude Stein Explains"
The Antioch Review: "Moose at Dusk, Western Montana"
Witness: "Patience"
Nimrod: "Sargent in Hawaii"
Western Humanities Review: "Adam Asks a Favor," "I Took the Photographer to Italy," "At the Agnes Martin Exhibition," "Self Portrait as Elegy," "Returning to My Father's Office," "Identifying the Body"
Whetstone: "Promised Land," "Song of the Horizontal"
Hubub: "Amelia Earhart Speaks from the Grave"
Maryland Poetry Review: "Prayer at Passover"
The Madison Review: "Disappearances"
North Carolina Literary Review: "Imperfect Sonnet for Richard"
The Louisville Review: "Elegy in Three Museum Visits"

Contents

III.

"We can't stop now. I thought I'd stop when it was going well. But now it's going very badly. It's too late. We can't stop now."

Alberto Giacometti while painting a portrait of James Lord

The Brain — is wider than the Sky —
for — put them side by side —
The one the other will contain
With ease — and You — beside

The Brain is deeper than the sea —
For— hold them — Blue to Blue—
The one the other will absorb —
As Sponges — Buckets — do

The Brain is just the weight of God —
For — Heft them — Pound for Pound
And they will differ — if they do —
As Syllable from Sound —

Emily Dickinson

for my mother, Edwina Davis

in memory of my father, Jerome Davis

and for my husband, Paul Bogas, *always* . . .

one

Adam Asks a Favor

Wait, don't make her yet.
Before she takes the sound
of wind into her mouth,
before her moving shape
shapes my waking, before
her perfect instep marks
this garden's end, before
my pulse starts its screaming,
I need to ask you this.
I have a feeling. Promise
me she'll be more flowers
than trees, more fish than sea.
Don't let her be too much
me or you or the word
that binds us; don't tell
her our family name. Give
her a voice less certain
than wanting. Curl her hair
as the morning glories curl
each morning. Widen her eyes
but shorten her fingers.
Make sure she understands,
I am the difference. If
you wait to make her while
I sleep you'll have the best
view of my dream. I want her
to be what I need her to be,
not me, but a picture of me.

My Husband Saying Kaddish

The first time I mistook it for a headache —
his fingers spread across closed eyes,
rocking heel to toe. Moving in close I heard
his prayer, mumbled, foreign, intimate,
between Paul and the forces of celestial nature
that might compel the small boat carrying
his delicate mother and wide-eyed father
across the black river and into heaven. It's his job,
he does it dutifully. For 11 months and a day
he recites his recommendation: *please see*
to their safe arrival, there are no better citizens,
what they did for me deserves eternal peace.

Who can you petition with prayer? In another
world, in another language, Agamemnon stood
on the shore of the mockingly still Aegean,
held up his baby daughter Iphigenia, begged
for a maelstrom — a deaf drone of whirl, crash
and lethal rain to carry his warships to Troy,
to Priam, to battle: *my girl's worth having, leave*
survival up to me, war is glorious, war is hell.

Years ago, my daughter only a set of dividing
cells within me, Paul and I woke up one morning
before dawn in Venice, Italy. In silence we rolled
our bags to the end of a short, empty pier,
shifting our weight as the fog closed in
and the water rang the dockbells. A boat roared
into view. We rode backwards all the way home
(a world away) to the evening fog of West Virginia.
High above the Atlantic, we piled our hands
onto my belly and said our prayer: *a child please,*
healthy and bright who will love us and care
for us, we will do our best to lift, to carry
this child across the rising dark water. . .

At the Agnes Martin Exhibition

It wasn't foul weather that chased
me in here but a long assault of black
limousines, a hearse at the start.
I'm not superstitious. Truly,
I don't know what to do about
the grieving. I've lost my faith
in consolation. Consolation but not

geometry. Clean lines make good company.
Ammons says, *The form enables a self
becoming,* but I say form is a self
unbecoming. I say form allows
the grieving their grief. Form is my
shoulders shouldering up this
first autumn after my father's death.

Form is the shape of my grace. I bake
pies for their roundness, I stack
photographs by size. Every morning
I measure coffee in heaping teaspoons
and sleep by the circles under my eyes.
I soap up one leg and down the other.
I write sonnets to save space.

So it was faith that brought me
to these window-size grids awash
in grieving tones. Look — it's my
childhood meadow in ecstasy: the canvas
that stretches from the shoulder of every
Michigan highway in May. Fields of color —
larkspur blue, wild ginger white, the pure

pink of partridgeberry. From a distance
this saturation is motion, a whole
wide meadow blooming. But closer up
each canvas is a single petal under
the microscope — the surface magnified
so its weave of veins and time matches
the weave of veins and time on my

hands. Patterns blend. I feel almost
regular. Still, the old woman had
an awful need to sanctify. She named
these pictures after the trees of Eden
and desert flowers, fantastic or
divine. Actually, there are no
flowers figured here, no recognizable

forms, just clean lines undoing
into petal, color, wash and grid.
Yet these canvases all say to me:
here is your geometry, your consolation,
grace. Make this your sacred place,
perfect cemetery. Stay here and be
yourself, *myself*, unbecoming in grief.

Patience

I should be glad for this mossy rock,
a dry night's rest, your long body

next to me, days of mountainscape left.
I might remark, this is what I hoped

Montana would look like: miles of darkest
green. And empty, the inconsolable chased

away by the starless skies. I expected
to see you happy here, bounding between

the intrepid sameness of each leafy rise.
If only I hadn't spent the afternoon

scanning the rooted trail for your
mud prints and phantom markings. All

I asked was *when* and you were gone,
quicker than the water that chases rain.

I would thank you for bringing me
to this exact place (how did you know?),

but you're already breathing the
melodic breath, the righteous breath

of the man who lead me up the wrong
side of a mountain so as not to say

he would (yes, would) love me one day.
You're dreaming. I could read an entire

book or write one, my eyes are so wide open.
Sleep is not the only thing I wait for.

Promised Land

I've been there: north of Galilee,
the shallow end of the Mediterranean
shores against weathered white stone.

At three in the afternoon they
released us from the avocado fields
and we stripped as we walked —

first shirts, then shorts, finally
shoes and hats — and dove as one
towards the bruised sun rounding

west. It was a beaten path, over
abandoned railroad tracks, past
the U.N. peace keepers patrolling

the Lebanese border. I could, I
have, walked that way in the dark,
my eyes closed. The night before

leaving I wanted to be alone
and swim out from and back to
those rocks, that path, the even

rows of avocado trees. Geography
matters. Ten years later and that
landscape is mapped on the inside

of my lover's hands. Yes, I smell
salt air when he presses me flat
to the mattress and, yes, I think

of scrub sage when he places his
large hands on the small of my back.
When he puts his mouth to my neck

and sings my name and *tesoro*,
I'm sure I've been returned
to the silent edge of the shallow

end of the bluest sea, where my
sweat ran off and the future
floats. It is the memory of having

been somewhere and seen myself
reflected, and to feel that same
rhythm in the voice of a gentle

man, in his hands as they run
the length of me repeating,
ti ho travata. Lost; recovery.

He Caught Everything

My father wrote valentines left-handed,
played racquet sports and ate peanuts

right-handed, operated on the left eye
with his left hand, the right eye with

his right hand. Once during a fondue party,
the kitchen caught fire. My father, using

both hands, carried the burning pot through
the back door, down the porch steps, across

the yard and into the garage. They had to
use a scalpel to pry his hands from the metal.

Advice to an Insomniac

Some things to do when you cannot sleep:
match shoes to hats or socks to socks, try
counting your gloves, the single ones you keep

piled behind letters that are easy to keep
but hard to remember. Reread Northrop Frye.
Some things to do when you cannot sleep!

Chant these names until you fall asleep:
grandmother, mother, aunt, sister. Cry
for the distance between you. Keep

listening for the blackbirds that fly
into the cottonwoods. Their songs die
at dawn while other musicians sleep.

Notice what the sleeping never see. My
friend, you are lucky enough to spy
on the world as it dreams, as it weeps.

I know, I do this every night: I lie
awake imagining the darkening sky.
Something I do when I cannot sleep:
hold fast to the things I cannot keep.

The Hasids from my Window

They are garment men, schmatta merchants,
"in the rag trade," my grandfather would say.
I know they are waiting for ordinary things:

truckloads of size 14 dresses in time for Easter.
Yet, the courage of their leaning makes me
breathless — when they stretch perpendicular

to the building, one hand gripping the window
frame, the other arched over bottle-thick glasses,
surveying the open road. It was in this posture

(swaying with anticipation) that they looked past
me each Friday evening, towards the setting sun,
as if some light might glance the coat of the

hurrying messiah, on his way around the corner.

Backpacking in Early Spring: Portrait of Your Husband Missing You

He said, "I'd be happy just watching her walk,"
and jumped ten feet to the next boulder, his boots
leaving regular marks of orange dust on the white
surface. "Grace," he continued, "watch her move,

she moves like water." Not the winter water that wanders
up the shallow roots of prickly pear; not the water
sloshing in his pack; not even the teasing water
of the spring storm clouds that gather and move on.

But the water that drips from his temples onto
the honey mesquite blooms, making the petals shine.
It's the water his own body rushes back into itself;
the water streaming into his eyes — myopia water —

distorting this desert, making whatever is dry
and distant, drier, more distant. It's the water
that glosses his thorn-scratched calves and his sun
burned neck; the water he spits on a wayward toad

like manna; the water he leaves with thumb-prints
like a talisman on the map. *He was here.* It's the water
in his eyes waking with the Big Dipper bearing down
on a vision of you, asleep, your dark hair fanning

your bird-bone fingers. It's the water of his loneliness:
loving someone so brilliant and knowing you might
not always be; or worse; you might not always be his.

To Cassius Clay in Detroit, 1961

Later that year, unbeknownst to the press, Cassius Clay drove from Miami to
Detroit to hear Elijah Muhammad address a mass meeting for the first time.
The trip took on added importance when, in Detroit, Clay met Malcolm X.
— Thomas Hauser,
Muhammad Ali: His Life and Times

I. Joe Louis

This is the city of copper rivers and runaway men,
the start of the jab and lean, punch and duck.
Some gestures remain: thick necks bent over assembly lines,
the slow-moving parts of the American dream.
Their heads jerk back when whistles blow, foremen scream.

Before your shuffle, dance and float, the Bomber stalked
this shifting sludge, this northern end of the underground
line — escape route, relief. This is the city of bridges back
from freedom. There is Canada. And there are the rivers
of buried gold: gloves, medals, the championship belt.

II. Malcolm X

Now, now the new one has come
to lift the bowed heads,
open sealed throats,
pitch a gathered scream,
and straighten you out,
stand you tall, change
all of our names!
Stroked by his God
your wings break out —
and you float yourself to glory.

Motherless

My friend from birth,
Hannah, and my husband,

they wake in the silver
dawn each day, heft

the swollen wool of early
spring over their heads,

stretching fingers through
the hand-knit sleeves,

pull on a boot at a time,
trudge through the forest,

humming in the blue dark,
the swaying canopy lightening

into day, the dew a disappearing
shroud of lace. At the well they

throw their buckets down,
the crash of metal on stone

is a lullaby of emptiness.

Romeo Gets There First

He was surprised by all that snow —
the topiary drifts banking the golden
path shot through with riotous
roses, perpetual phlox.

There were naked children
who fell down laughing and came up angels,
their gay relief still moving
in the after light of tiny arms

and tiny legs gone running off.
Even the heavy branches of the evergreens
(of course this place would be full of trees)
were welcoming. No danger here. No cold?

So it took two ruined
snowmen before he understood his own heat.
The pitiful coal and carrot stick
slushing in the car-less street

just after he walked by. *Searing,*
he thought, *I'm on fire.*
By the time he reached the forest
(so hot and sweaty) and stood in the center

of the center-most grove calling
and calling her name,
the place was awash in formless flakes.
And since she had to wake from her dream

of death and stab herself for good; time
(yes, it passes even here)
made first a storm of the frosted leaves
and then a frantic river

running into a deepening lake. And soon
he had melted an ocean's worth
of celestial snow and
was drowning there in heaven's wake.

Amelia Earhart Speaks from the Grave

It happens just after sunrise
    when the ground is yellow and the sky shines violet.
       My father is sitting sideways on his bed, facing the window.
Because his eyes don't focus it is impossible to know
    if he is looking through the window or simply facing it. For
       the first time in months he is motionless. Still.
He doesn't pucker his lips into a circle and gently push
    his tongue through and through. He doesn't rub the tips
       of his fingers with his thumb. His feet are turned parallel
and balanced on a stuffed bunny that has fallen to the floor. He is not
    an old man, but he looks old — his skin loose
       around his visible bones. His body is stiff and bent forward
like an antenna receiving a signal. He keeps his eyes
    closed. Around him the pale green walls of the nursing home
       reflect the morning light as it fades. Everyone else is
sleeping or turning over in the moment before waking. It is now
    that my father hears her. He stands up quickly and leans
       his ear to the window, stretching his arms like
airplane wings. The glass shakes in its frame. This is the moment: my
    father, language having left him to silence only months ago,
       turns to give Amelia's message to his wife who is standing
in the doorway, waiting to feed him breakfast. "The water," he says,
    "is all around me. No room to fly."

Sargent in Hawaii

Forget the improbable passage,
the cumbersome clothing,
the expense, the unfamiliar food, the infections.
Consider the possibilities —
obviously of light,
but also of noble profiles,
of seamless seas.
Think of how he loved Capri —
its brown skinned girls in native dress bending trees
to their playful ways.
A single braid involved more
brush strokes then several boats,
foliage and fruit.
The Hawaiian girls would have
it made with their blue-black hair
and their skin the color
of late autumn leaves.
Poor John would surely be up nights
trying to show how the Hawaiian girls don't just sleep
but deeply dream.
And fruit is different there,
not like fruit at all
but more like secret flesh,
the stockinged thighs of a diplomat's daughters.
Such bright heaven.

Once I dreamed that Sargent feared
the water and kept his distance
from the beach. That makes sense on Capri
where the land is rock and twigs,
never confused with the sea.
But in Hawaii everything is water —
lilies, turtles, bare-bottomed children, even trees.
You can't escape it,
not by brush or bottle.
It's every way you walk.
The mountains dissolve into water.
The sky is an equal green.

The painter wound up paralyzed, motionless and wrapped
in dry white fabric searching
the ground for a tunnel home.
But, that was just my dream.
We all know Sargent loved boats
(if gondolas count)
and the view across foreign water.
We all know he could make a paradise of anything, socialites
on sofas or a children's game.
Consider the tropics of
Carnation, Lily, Lily, Rose —
its whirlpool of grass,
tidal wave of watery light,
its isolation and tranquility.

Disappearances

Sometimes I have the simplest dream:
my father, in a parka and boots, holding

a red shovel, is waving from an ice floe
somewhere in the Arctic. He is blowing

kisses as he drifts towards the pole's sun-lit
curve. My father kept two picture postcards

on the wall above his desk. The smaller
was a color reproduction of Brueghel's

"Fall of Icarus." Along the curving
mountainside, a farmer sows seeds,

while peasants dance a harvest jig.
The sea angles from the top left corner

to the bottom right where two feet
and several feathers mark the land's end.

On the back, in my father's hand is written,
"see me." The other was a black and white

photograph of Amelia Earhart in the cockpit
of her Lockheed Electra, on the morning

before she missed tiny Howland Island
and was lost over the Pacific. She is waving

and smiling. My brother thinks my father
admired Earhart's fearlessness, or maybe

he was in love with her. But I think he wanted
to be her, in the moment the water closed

around all but her ankles and her wings
resurfaced. I keep both postcards in a book

called *Ring of Bone* by Lew Welch, not because
he was a poet of distinction but because

he was last seen walking into the foothills
of the Sierras with a shotgun and a tambourine.

Elegy in Three Museum Visits
Margaret McCormick Brown 1965–1998

I. The National Gallery

Everybody coughs. Nobody is sick, but nobody
is comfortable. The new wing is overheated
and the line for the Cambodian show is a wave
of disrobing tourists: smashed hats, unknotted
scarves, shoulders raised against a collar.
Winter in Washington is a burden of hefted wool.
I'm smart and under-dressed. The gallery is dark

and cold then warm with spotlights trained
on slender brown statues carved from nut-wood
trees that root above ground. My hands are empty
but they are not free. I struggle not to touch.
How I want to swipe a single finger down a broad
nose, cup a curved buttock, press my two hands
to one of the nine offered up by the dancing

goddess of fortune. All these bodies in mad
release — elephant heads on adolescent torsos,
ageless men with bowed necks and straight spines
holding the lotus position for eternity. I can't
bear the lidless eyes stuck in unfocused abandon,
seeing everywhere. It's February, you've lost
a breast. I shiver and hold my own hand.

II. The Mattress Factory

Too late to spare you
the silver gloom
of a Midwestern March.
You've seen this before,
lightless sky in a sky-less
city. Sad, but not too sad.
You said, *Minneapolis*
is not like Paris but
it's a good enough place
to die. I said *Be grateful*
you're not in Pittsburgh.
You laughed but I didn't
mean it. You see, my dear,
in Pittsburgh, in March
with your best friend
beside, you can cross
a short bridge over
unmoving water and touch
the night sky. I'm talking
about Turrell's "Pleiades,"
(those seven sad stars)
it's a long dark room built
for two and nothingness.
Constellations give way —

Oh Maggy, when I was Osiris
dismembered by grief
you gathered me up
piece by undone piece.
You said, *I remember you.*
You said, *This is your hand,*
now reach. But, touch
isn't love. We are held
together with light not heat.

III. The Whitney

On the way in I heard an older man say,
Did you know that in Houston, Rothko has his own
chapel, named for his paintings, not for him
but called The Rothko Chapel all the same.
A younger man, maybe a friend, responded,
It's small, suffused with light and empty
except for some wood benches and a triptych
of very black, very late paintings.
Their companion, a girl dressed like a woman, added,
You know, towards the end of his life
Rothko wanted to use less color and eventually
all his paintings, even if he included purple
or blue, turned out black. They all look black.

If you can forgive the early portraiture
(and you should) Rothko is that simple:
there was color, (huge blinding blocks of it)

and then there was black. Orange pooled into red,
purple mounted gray and yellow came from other
yellow. Squares mutated into rectangles, nothing
bled the frame. And then there was black.
The older man, the younger man and the girl
in women's clothing, always two paces ahead of me,
are reassured. She says, *See, and then he died.*
Indeed, there is less and less color, but less
and less color is actually less and less paint.
(I got up close and looked so hard I felt it.)

And less paint allows for more light. More light,
how perfect. So it is that simple. At the end,
it wasn't what Rothko wanted us to see, it's what
he wanted us to see into. Into light. Such light.
But, Maggy, what I want in this nearly empty
gallery, in this overly air-conditioned museum,
on this day long past Easter Sunday (the day you
died), isn't to see into Rothko's dying light.
What I want is to see through, all the way through.

two

Of Radio, Ballet, and Space Travel: Suite for a Woman, Not Me

I. Awake: Gathering Sound

Mine was a thunderous apprenticeship.
In the park, alone, on a bright Sunday.
I went out to gather sound. That's what
radio people call it, gathering sound.
The day was practically an October cliché:
trees on the edge of turning gold, or igniting
red, the air was truly crackling and Rock
Creek babbled nearby. I had to concentrate
to keep my hands from reaching out for rough
bark, or shiny river stones. I wanted to sing,
or dance. I felt like Gene Kelly. Well,
Gene Kelly wearing headphones and carrying
a microphone, weighted down with a DAT machine
and several cables. Okay, so it would have been
impossible to actually dance. Not to mention
ridiculous. Besides, the first time you hear
the world mic'd in stereo you can't do anything
but stand still, as in is-this-God-I'm-hearing
still. Statue still. It's the sound of heavenly
voices broken into a thousand individual lights,
each light caught like a bug in a tiny glass jar.
It's unbearable. I closed my eyes. A storm
gathered on the ground. The loudness makes you
jump. At first you're trying to hush the noise,
or run from it. Then, of course, you realize that
you are making the damn noise. And since it's you,

well, me, then hell, I had to listen: the crunch
of a leaf, no many leaves, no someone walking
across the leaves. Okay, me, I'm walking across
the leaves. There's the boom of my own foot
coming down on something insignificant — an acorn
or a lost coin — and sounding like Godzilla
laying Manhattan to waste. Toe, heel, crunch,
crack, shatter, scatter. I can hear each bird song
frozen into individual notes. Caw, trill, caw.
Then there is water, a creek with a menacing roar.
I could drown if I got too close, imagine white
water surging between rocks, the perfect storm.
Like I said, it's loud. Any innocent creek,
winding its unimpressive way through a city park
becomes an imposing ocean. Next I hear the wind —
it's deafening. I need to hold on to something,
anything, a tree, a bench or it will undoubtedly
carry me out of Kansas, but oh no, I'm not in
Kansas anymore. After the tornado there is traffic.
What's the plural of whoosh? Between the road
and the river, what was distinct now converges.
Traffic, walking, wind, water. Tire, shift,
rumple, slip, rustle, bounce, splash, gurgle,
sink, hush, hush, hush. My ears were new spoons.

II. Dreaming: Muscle Memory

Once I had been the child
        who studied long,
    who knew enough
of the tension running

up the back of my thigh
        connecting the arc
    of my shoulders
with the curve of my neck,

the near-fall balance
        of my imperfect
    arabesque. I didn't think
to point my toes, tilt my

pelvis up, breathe in three
        four time. I didn't
    have to think, my body
knew. I could do this in my

sleep. Awake, my legs extended
        thoughtlessly in front
    of every reflective
surface, mirrors of course,

but oven fronts as well,
        store windows,
    even the two-way glass
at police headquarters.

(I walked by on my way to
        class every day.)
As a child, I was liquid
poured in a hurry or never

poured, pooled instead in
        a small spoon.
I was the model statue.
But moving, I was another

tempest brewing, scientists
        call it shape
memory: heat any
metal and bend it into any

shape, then let it cool.
        Heat it again and it
resumes the first, original,
shape. Little girls listen to

their own design. I quit
        for the same reason
everyone quits. I was
good, but not good enough.

III. Awake: Space

I'll try to explain. It's like having a dull dream
about your job when suddenly the spoon you used
to eat your soup at lunch grows Alice in Wonderland
huge and offers itself as a brace for the sagging
limb of the talking tree. What? Exactly.
Once I went up in a NASA rocket. Seriously.
I wore a space suit with my name signatured across my heart.
I carried an airsick bag and my recording equipment.
The cool part was experiencing weightlessness.
It takes you by surprise. I mean you think you're prepared,
you wait for it, expect it and then WHAM
your arms just fly up over your head like a woman flagging
down a bus after an accident. And you can't lower them for trying.
You ascend. Did you read that Gabriel Garcia Marquez novel?
The one where the woman is so beautiful that one day
while doing laundry she just rises up to heaven.
I rose up. The next time I tried to be in control,
pretended I was floating like those astronauts you see on TV
waving and mouthing "hi mom" into the camera.
But here's the Alice in Wonderland part —
in my effort to float I managed, somehow, and I swear
I don't know how, to strike this balletic pose from my childhood.
Is that a word, balletic? Anyway, it was like involuntary dancing.

My arms lifted above my head to third position and my legs
reached out in a surprisingly well executed grand jete.
I'm not making this up. I wouldn't know how.
There I was a god-damn baby swan. And the part I left out,
the part that's hard to explain, is that when the rocket turns
the corner out of weightlessness your body feels like it's twice
as heavy as it actually is and you're thrown to the floor
as if you were struck on the back by a whole, huge, felled tree.
Well, not me. No, I was a reincarnated Pavlova and I simply sunk
down in dramatic collapse like, what else — a dying swan.
You're wondering how I can be sure, I was on a rocket after all,
thinking about radio recordings. Okay, so NASA videotaped
the flight and I watched the video, but that's not how I knew.
That's just how I confirmed what I already knew. The thing is,
I could hear myself dancing (if that's what you call it)
while that rocket was going in and out of weightlessness.
It sounded like nothing I had ever heard through a stereo microphone
before: my eyes opening, chin jutting, fingers fluttering, neck
craning, knees locking, toes pointing. Lift, fly, fall.
Then silverware crashing, crashing, crashing.

three

Once Again to *Falling Water*

Engaged, we moved north to West Virginia. We bought
a house, our first, and dug in. Winter came early

and white. The house was newly built and ordinary
but we loved the view: in-town and half way up a hill.

Mostly, we saw lights and trees. We took our time
choosing a marriage bed — settling on a warm oak

sleigh with mismatched antique night tables. We hung
your grandmother's tiny water-color of Russian willows

in the entryway. I learned to cook. We put out the good
china with the goblets my mother found in her attic.

We entertained, stayed in. When visitors came from far
away, we took them to see the overlook at Cooper's Rock

and then an hour into Pennsylvania to Frank Lloyd Wright's
masterpiece, *Falling Water*. "The most famous private

home in America." Take the tour ten times and you too
will know this and more: the house was commissioned

by the Kaufmans, of Kaufmans department store in Pittsburgh.
The Kaufmans were rich, but they were not tall. Thank god.

Because, according to our guides, Wright believed anyone
over five feet seven was a weed. The ceilings are hardly

any higher. Our first time there you had to stoop to get
from room to room. Wright designed all of the furniture

and linens for *Falling Water*, except a set of hand-carved
dining chairs that came from Tuscany. If I close my eyes

I can hear Mrs. Kaufman saying sternly, "It's my house,
I live here." She must have truly loved those chairs.

Once, when the guide headed upstairs, I caught you running
your hand across the double cushioned ottoman. "Sittable,"

you whispered, nodding your head with approval. Driving
home, I imagined myself living there. I wouldn't walk

but glide across the slate floor polished to practical
wetness and recline languidly on the sofas upholstered

in fabrics the color of sunsets. I'd be at home among
such unassuming geometry. I might spend an entire day

in the second floor study, opening and closing the corner
window, letting in the sound of the waterfall then shutting

it out, then letting it in again. The water falls
a modest distance; but the house nearly falls over

the water. In bed after our first visit you suggested,
"Let's cantilever." Wright would often drop in unannounced

to check that each pillow was in its correct place,
that nothing offensive had wandered into view.

And to check on the view itself which I hadn't noticed
until the last time when our brand new guide, Tom,

an architecture student, gleefully pointed out
the windows. "They are perfect Wrightian rectangles,"

he paused to let the "perfect" part sink in. Indeed,
they are longer than they are tall. They sit high

in the wall, high enough that if you're standing,
looking out, you cannot see the ground, but not too high

because you cannot see the sky either. "Wright wanted you
to see nothing but green vista." Southeastern Pennsylvania

is rich in Appalachian green. In spring, those hills
are smeared a hypnotizing forest which fades to a

comfortable kelly in summer, deepening to avocado
skin by November. Then the green goes dormant, curling

in from the edges, so only the center spine of the holly
leaves speak of green. And winter makes, well, wintergreen.

Years later (yesterday) and several states away
from West Virginia or Pennsylvania, I was lying

on the acupuncturist's table, looking sideways
through her window at the rectangle of black trees.

I couldn't see one entire tree, just several lovely
curves where the heaviest branches sway from the trunk

and spread away. I could see some branches completely,
others were cut off mid-knot or twist or sprouting.

It was the original winter view from *Falling Water* —
the sleeping panorama of shivering trees, their leafless

limbs weary with waiting for the light to change.
Then, early this morning I woke up in our current house

with our toddler asleep in the next room, two red robins
shocking against the snow in the mulberry tree outside

our bedroom window. You were burrowed deep beneath
the blanket beside me. I lifted the covers stealthily,

to look, finally, to see — you — my sleeping husband,
my bear in season, my constant view, my green vista.

I Took the Photographer to Italy

because all summer he shot me naked
with only the yard — kiddie pool, tomato
plants, recycling bins — as background.
Worse, he never allowed me to look directly

into the camera; he thought my stare too
ordinary; "somewhere far off please, you
are my Madonna." It wasn't the flattery
but the distortion that made me glare.

Because every morning I would offer him my
shyest features — my hands, my ankles —
to hold, to kiss, and he would shake his head,
saying, "Too small." I took the photographer

to Italy so he could see Botticelli's Venus,
her long fingers spread against her chest, her
eyes averted, one pupil higher than the other,
unparalleled. Even bending, he could not meet

her gaze. In the Vatican we stood before an
unsigned Virgin, the child suckling, her left
eye looking east towards a star, her right eye
wandering west, lost. I took the photographer

to Florence to see the Medici chapel with
Michelangelo's secret charcoal drawings behind
plexiglass in the basement. Studies for grand
things, they are quick, eye-level sketches of

papal feet, the hands of a king. Somewhere,
taller than the photographer, taller than the tall
Danish tourist hiding his camera, taller even
than Michelangelo himself, was a single pair

of furiously drawn, lashless eyes, staring up.
Underground, pressed together, in the buzzing,
unnatural light, against those heavy lines
("So certain," he said, "as if the charcoal

never left the surface,") the photographer
saw my actual size, able to reach around
his life and hold him steady in my eyes, he
knew my love was huge, unblinking, unmediated.

Self Portrait as Elegy

In the white light of any given Texas day
I look just like you: dark hair from darker

hair; connected lobes; a jawline squared
by Cossacks and night grinding. These are

your eyes: semitic circles beneath heavy
lids, heavier brows. This afternoon's headache

is your intolerance for wet heat. My short
fingers press against the temples of my

inheritance. There is no relief in the un-
ruined cathedral of the immigrant mind.

And in the domed black of every Texas night
I look even more like you: awake and wandering

from the window to the mirror to the shelf,
from the dark to my own reflection to toys

you brought home from your office, magnifying
glass and prisms, angling them towards

the light you'd chant, *refraction, refraction*:
to break back the light to break back

the brightest light. But survival looks
nothing like daybreak or any other dawning.

It looks like the empty night folded into
losses where constellations of silver stars

spin out your name, my future, my hope.

Prayer at Passover

Sleeplessness is dry. My body only bones,
light enough to balance on the tapered tip
of a cactus spike. Myself a cactus dowsing

for dreams like winter's water. My teeth
ache. My mouth stings. I curse inaccessible
peace. Gladly I'd relinquish this: my tongue

(ugly and thick). I'd promise only promises
kept. You, then, must deliver me into drowsy
death, the sleep of the guileless, facing up.

I know it comes by your outstretched hand, not
by flood, or a fiery angel. Yet even the tiniest
cactus, each spring, offers at least one flower,

searing orange to shame the sun. One bright burning
bush. Apology for the year's harsh armor? Yes.
And atonement for needing such lethal protection.

Returning to My Father's Office

Oh no, not this room.
I can't bear the ophthalmoscope,
thick and solid like a sturdy tree — upright and alone.
Once I felt safe here, cradled
among the wall charts and vision
instruments, the tools of the conjurer.

I always considered my father a conjurer.
Every day in this room,
a line of people would come and go, some seeing,
some not quite. They'd climb into the ophthalmoscope,
he would shine his light. Did they feel cradled
or did they feel alone?

When he died, all I felt was alone.
I searched this office; conjured
its windowless dark; its antiseptic smell; its cradle
of blue light. A shadow-filled room,
his lonely ophthalmoscope,
his immaculate chamber, his vision.

There is a new doctor now, he can't see
my father. What does he know? He thinks he is alone.
He thinks this is his ophthalmoscope!
I know better; he is no conjurer.
This is not his examining room.
He can't cradle

refraction — break back the light through the cradle
of beveled glass magnifying the vision
chart low on the north wall of this room.
I close my eyes, pretend I'm alone,

I am the conjurer,
on this throne, this ophthalmoscope!

Yes, in this magical chair, my father's ophthalmoscope,
I spin the radiant handles, turn this cradle
until he appears, I will conjure
my lost father, and see
what I always saw here. I am not afraid to be alone,
in his examining room.

With this ophthalmoscope, I am the visionary.
Cradled by my childhood, I see the future: myself alone,
but the other conjurer, my father, is in me in this room.

September 11th, One Year After

The truth is I cleaned out my closets.
I had the radio on, two radios actually,
one in the kitchen and one in the bedroom,
the names ringing out in stereo
as I discarded broken-limbed umbrellas,
sad single mittens, receipts loosed
from upended purses. I found surprising solace
in the methodical turning of hanger heads,
folding of woolen sweaters in anticipation
of true winter. I discovered an old friend's
band jacket rumpled in the back, "Mandy" mowed
into the tall grass of the Cyrillic,
varsity-sized B. (For Boylestown? Bishop?)
There were my daughter's snow boots,
the ones she wore only once, on my birthday,
when we took the typical photographs,
the three of us laughing and pointing
into the propped up camera, our snowman
(with an actual carrot nose) standing stout
in front. But the film was loaded wrong,
the pictures never took. I cradled those shiny
red boots in my lotus lap as I lined up
the others — the worn, scuffed, loved
shoes — in careful rows of two all headed west
towards an invisible arc (O rescue.)
At 8:48 I was finished with the front hall
and headed for my husband's closet still clutching
Bella's boots. A bell chimed, two bells chimed,

one in the kitchen and one in the bedroom.
I stopped in the hallway and there it was,
the memory of last year before I knew:
my baby daughter, whose name is the word
for beautiful as well as the word for war,
standing at the picture window preparing
to wave good bye. My leaving was always
easy. But that day, for the first time,
she clung to me, her cries of "no, no, no"
ringing around the living room and I thought,
What's wrong? Downtown, in DC, her father
climbed the marble stairs to his government
office and the sky filled with planes.

Moose at Dusk, Western Montana

in response to a poem by Mona Van Duyn

This is the writing hour: the cool evening
of light and dark. I am riding the back
of a motorbike, returning from the Rocky
Mountain Front. The place, my lover said,
where this is surely that. Where the most

gray of the stoney gray mountains give way,
suddenly, to prairie grass ("an ocean's worth").
My lover said every poet should stand with
a toe in each: warm wheat and cold rock.
I stood, I even turned my face to the sun.

Nothing moved without the wind. Nothing
hopped, scampered, or slithered by. Snow
melted. Amber waved. What poetry? What this?
But here, off the shoulder of highway 12,
between Lost Gulch and the Valley of Praise,

comes a she-moose, barely brindled, blinking
and thirsty. She drinks from the spring
run-off collected in the ditch. She is huge,
spindly, and oblivious to us. She is not
grand against the leaning pines; she is not

matched. She is perfectly proportioned.
Behind her a red squirrel scatters needles
and broken twigs. A thrush jay changes
branches; the brown tree-snake tightens
its hold. Monarchs alight. We sit still.

Oh my Montana, where evening comes without
pencils, without perspective, without calm.
Where the she-moose comes before the full
dark, beneath the gathering storm and beside
the highway, where we are neither this nor that
but just us, just so.

Where Are You, Denis Johnson?

Roll over, press your ear to the new grass.
It's me, *beautiful Susan*, your lady of the wet
heavy heat of Houston. Yes, everything has melted
so I need to ask,
                            it it true?
Have you gotten married? Rumor has you high
in the mountains of Idaho, high enough to breathe
cool air as light as lace. I'm beginning to think
it's a phenomenon I'll
                            never know
again, trapped as I am in the seething hold
of Texas. Texas once dry as all good dust, crumbling
rust and cracked cactus. All of which has blurred
to this: Whitman waving
                            as we ride
the bus. The street could be what? The Mojave,
Mississippi, Kansas prairie. It's the downtown we can't
bear to wander through for fear of empty mouths,
blank faces or worse
                            smut and garbage
piling up; our children won't imagine the highways
that connect suburbia with everything their parents
forgot — the song that travels from darkness
to what will be
                            from morning
to night or another in between; from the old world
across every blue body of water to possibility. Yes,
the distance is the thing — Whitman waving to you,
me, and our America.

On the Close

Somewhere between the Cathedral and the tennis courts
I lost my favorite necklace, the one my mother gave
             me when I chose to teach: a silver square
                          with a raised lightning bolt and *listen*
etched in deep. It dangles from a black silk chord.
       Little goes missing here.
             Occasionally, home-made flyers appear asking
                   for the return of math books, gym socks, flute
cases, lipstick, journals.
                    I marshaled a posse of junior creative writers,
             girls in low slung jeans, shoulder-baring tops
and flip flops (the dress code be damned!) We took off in teams
       of two, their boyfriends'
             signet rings suddenly catching then letting go
then catching the capital light as it reigned across
       rose bushes and manicured lawns. My students take
             the search to heart. Meg and Hilda, the oddballs
in violet nail polish and knee socks, share peppermint gum.
       They assess the risk of reaching into the thorns;
             Jessica and Carlen argue for the righteousness
of a certain Anime character. Tough Sara tugs on her sleeves
                          and scowls. Trailing behind, dreamy
       Bridget collects decaying blooms, echoes
                          the birdsongs. Conscientious
Mariel, lets out a cry, "Oh my," and a gasp, "look: shoes!"

One red, one black, both patent-leather, worn
down at the heels but shiny around the buckle. To me they look
like a child's size, perhaps a bird-boned
teenager. One of my babes? Or a friend. . .
Bridget bends, cups the ruby slipper and sing-songs
"Dorothy, oh Dorothy. . ." and mixing
her references, she shyly slips the shoe on and sighs, "too small."
Alex, regal in her own right, chuckles
"I guess you're not going to the ball."
Sara frees her left hand quickly and in a flash upends
the dark shoe and my wayward charm.
But the others of my beauties, not paying attention, have broken out
in song: *Somewhere over the rainbow. . .skies. . . are. . .blue. .*
Ah, the English teacher's bind —
as the metaphor arcs appropriately, extended to include
the dreams that you dare
to dream . . . really do come true . . .
Do I stop my young charges from collapsing
into each others arms
in a heap of shared cliché
(the evil to end all composition evils) or do I point out
the pot of gold you get when you give
up the prince and abandon yourself
to the tornado whirling by.

The First Wife's Lament in Late Winter

I met him around now,
at my cousin's sweet sixteen birthday party.
I was fifteen years old,
he was seventeen.

Before the sky changed to
this perpetual gray and the ground froze, he
died. The winds were still warm.
I am fifty five.

He left ten years ago.
I missed him then as if my lungs had been cut
from my throat. I could not
breathe. But death gives time

more heft then healing. Now
my sadness is not sudden but certain, this
old ache from a wound healed
but not healed. We had

three children. I *have* three
children. I share this with them: something of my
childhood as something of
theirs is not just lost

but irretrievable.
My youngest, she is reeling, her reference
buried, I offer her
what I remember

but she does not see her
self in my face. I have a good life, I would
not take him back if he
were alive. But who

will remember that I
was once young and pretty, and full of hope, lust,
confidence? Who knew me,
who? I am not his

widow, he had a wife.
I was his lover for twenty five years, I
was his friend. He came to
my house with lilies,

my mother thought he had a beautifully shaped head.

Song of the Horizontal

O may this recovery room recover me
the possibility
of being upright
on the beach, a pudgy child

on my hip, my arm stretched
pointing to the perfect
blue of the horizon,
the silver-seamed blue of Leonardo's

sad theory that the farther away
things are the more
blue they appear.
O may this recovery room recover

my upright view of the possibility
of being someone's
never blue mother,
the kind (like mine) who can veil

a dark horizon in the light of her
comfort, her protection,
who can stretch
blue twilight into brighter

blue morning. O may my heart soon
beat its slower,
steadier, childless
beat, recovered, impossibly blue.

Gertrude Stein Explains

Indeed, I fell in love with that woman
because of the way she wears a dress.
Because of the way she wears the night
on her dress and the dress on her shoulders.
Because the funnel of her fingers when she
smooths the dress's sleeves is a faucet
of new music. It's a fine, fat button of love,
and I plan to wear it as a long, new life.

Perverted Nocturne

I should mount
video cameras in the high corners
of my bedroom, point one east
through the window to catch
the night sky as it arcs silver
into the morning. The other three
fixed on me, in bed, awake.
I would be naked, with vegetables,
train the cat to use his tongue.
Why not star in my own movie?
Wasn't it Marilyn Monroe
who so desperately needed sleep,
succumbing finally, to barbiturates
and rum? Actually, I believe it was
Bobby Kennedy sent to ease her out
of reach. Not me, I'll talk to the papers,
tell them everything I know: how the mocking
birds gather in the pecan trees before
dawn, how they hum then scatter, lifting
a wing at a time and arc above me
into the morning. I'd look into the camera
wet my lips and smile, it's the night sky
and me, always starring.

Moonlanding, 1969

I remember it this way:
Detroit in July,
early evening, a breeze
stirring the maple trees.
I was upstairs in bed.
I hadn't expected the pain
of the injections —
a tidal ache pulling
back across my stomach
and flooding fast —
my legs, feet and fingers.
There was so much blood.
I hadn't expected the abortion

to hurt worse than giving birth.
I called out for my husband.
I listened for him moving
in the house. Silence.
Then, the kettle's whistle.
Opening the window,
I saw him on the front porch,
holding the baby's hand
and pointing towards the sky.
Up and down the block,
the neighbors were outside,
like sculpture, their hands
saluting over their eyes,
squinting at the moon.

I called out for my husband
again and an ice cream truck
came ringing around the block.

Imperfect Sonnet for Richard

If it were up to me to end this day
I know how it would go: I'd toss a blossom
of crepe myrtle on your knee. (I tend to slow
every already slow turning — you know me.)
Next I'd fill a cup with sea water and balance
it in your hand. I'd angle your chaise west
and say *wait*. The end would be simple: when
the light on the single flower is the light
on the captured ocean, that's it — my end.
But you, what would you do? You'd rush the west
with a hefty bag of peaches. (Oh the excess
of a whole bag full!) So what if the music
stops and you don't have a chair. Who cares?
You'd toss the peaches this way: up. And up
they would go then rain delight on every
other slowly-spinning, peachless night.

Sheva B'rachot: A New Translation

1. Please pass the wine.

Thank you.

2. We are grateful
for this canopy of private
light, this neon music,
this joining, this twist.

Thank you.

3. I am there
in the clouds
as the clouds cross
the blue-domed bulb
of your eyes. You nod
and pass your glass.

Thank you.

4. Never mind the sticker
burrs; lantana obscuring
the view from the back porch.
The yard's the yard: same
as when your father first
assembled the swing-set,
your mother spread
manure over the hydrangeas,
both blue and purple.

Our pleasure.

5. It's a new hut of palm fronds
and bent banana trees.
No, it's a bouquet of maple
branches and woven oak
leaves. Maybe it's his
grandmother's prayer
shawl folded twice
and knotted to a linden
line. It feels to me, like silk,
spun from unearthed
promises, at home in the
home of our making.

No, no, it's our pleasure.

6. Let her lead him back
behind this house and its well-kept
garden to the woods where things grow
spiney and green.
Let him hear the thrush jay's call
and sing it back to her.
Let them kick over mushrooms —
rubbing the silky undersides against
their cheeks and rolling mossy rocks
between their toes. Let them trade
the leaves of mimosa trees,
fingering the curves with their eyes closed,

making up names for the seed pods.
Let them learn that memory lives
where you plant it, and that it grows.
Let the rain come and the darkness and the morning.
Let them wake in a mist of their own making.
Let them stay and be happy.

Of course.

7. Let it never end. Better,
let it spread. Let there be kisses
of transcendental contagion,
a feverish force of more and more
and more togetherness. Let them
rise and break and heal and expire.
Let them find the cure
in the first and fifth and ninth
and last shared glass of wine.

You're welcome.

Identifying the Body

Thank you, but I just don't recognize
this shrunken man, the ashen skin so smooth,
so cold, frozen? Yes, and dark beneath the eyes.
See his jaw line, following it you lose
the squareness of mine, the symmetrical scheme,
the hope. This cannot be my father, no,
my father never slept so sound, never dreamed
a sadness so entrenched would let him go.

Yet, there is something familiar about the shape
of his head, perhaps the curve of the ear.
Oh, I know that ear, I've whispered "escape"
many times, cupping my hand, trying to appear
independent, resolved, when we would conspire
to live past his fate. Go ahead, start the fire.

The Endless Story

On the 17th day, Noah's wife went to the window
and saw only water and knew the world was lost.

On the 20th day, Noah's wife went to the window
and saw only the saturated trunk of a willow tree
bobbing between the water's surface and the water.

On the 28th day, Noah's wife went to the window
and saw the same saturated trunk of the same

willow tree bobbing between the surface and the sky
and she thought, the world could be saved. The world
could be saved. But no message was ever sent.

No one said: this is what deliverance will look like.
Pay attention. She had figured out that the curve
of her nose mirrored the curve of her spine and, not

coincidentally, the curve of the cypress tree out back.
She measured fabric by that tree. Perhaps by out-

stretched hand he meant the steadfast cypress,
its knobby branches bobbing now above the spreading
sea — barkless bones born up by a wave. The fruitless

false top a weathered palm, open and expecting.
She had learned to look for something. Maybe this.

Notes

"At the Agnes Martin Exhibition" is for Doug Larsen.

"Promised Land" is for Nicole Cuddeback.

"Backpacking in Early Spring" and "Gertrude Stein Explains" are for Marisa de los Santos.

"Of Radio, Ballet, and Space Travel" was inspired by events in the life of Gemma Hooley, although the voice is not meant to imitate hers. The poem is dedicated to my students at The National Cathedral School for Girls and, of course, to Gemma.

"Once Again to Falling Water" is for my husband, Paul Bogas.

"Prayer at Passover" is for Seth Hurwitz.

"On the Close" refers to the "campus" or grounds (called a Close) of the National Cathedral in Washington, DC.

"Imperfect Sonnet for Richard" is for Richard Lapin.

The Sheva B'rachot are a set of seven traditional blessings chanted at a Jewish wedding during which the bride circles the groom seven times.

"The Endless Story" is for Lesley Anne Hyatt.

Gratitude

My heartfelt thanks to my teachers and readers: Lynn Bloom, Peter Parshall, Nicholas Christopher, Edward Hirsch, Richard Howard, Adam Zagajewski, Fiona Wilson, Nicole Cuddeback, Greg Fraser, Seth Hurwitz, Pimone Triplett, Doug Larsen, Mark Caughey, Amy Storrow, Robin Reagler, Patty Seyburn, Nancy Johnson, Barney Kirby, Rob Content, Carol Kutzer, Beth Vesel and David Teague.

I'm indebted to the literary souls whose keen insight and wise words turned my manuscript into a book: Marisa de los Santos, Jim Harms, Eve Muller, Gina Hyams, Anne Burt and Paul Bogas.

Thanks too to Vern Rutsala and Tony Gorsline for making my dream come true (and for being two of the unsung heroes of American poetry) and to John Rosenthal and Michael Czeiszperger who paint with light.

This book would not exist without the continued support of my friends and family, true believers every one: Josh, Carisa and Amy Davis. The Crolls of California, the Zacks of Michigan, the Shulevitzes of Oregon and the Goldmans of Durham. Lesley Anne Hyatt, SJ Childs, Karen Belsey, Andrea Nakayama, Hannah Golub, Gemma Hooley, Stacey Greenwald, Evelyn Leong, Mark Hussey, Melissa Giraud, Sharon Goodman, Kevin Oderman, Sara Pritchard, the Cerbones, Beth Posner, Kelly Alexander, the Spielblocks, John Eastman, Ruth Mayer, Emily Hanford and Jonathan Kronstadt.

Bella and Milo Davis are my reasons to live and my reasons to write.

About the Publisher

Bedbug Press was founded in 1995 by Tony Gorsline, who has had a lifelong love of books and writing. Under the imprints Cloudbank Books and Fairweather Books, Bedbug Press has published ten books of poetry, a memoir, and a series of children's coloring books.

In 2003, the press established The Northwest Poetry Series with the publication of *My Problem with the Truth* by Chris Anderson. Since then three more books by Northwest poets have been added to the series: *Insects of South Corvallis* by Charles Goodrich, *Out of Town* by Lex Runciman, and *A Bride of Narrow Escape* by Paulann Petersen.

Also in 2003, the press began an annual poetry contest, The Rhea & Seymour Gorsline Poetry Competition. The contest offers a cash prize and publication of the winning manuscript. *Textbook Illustrations of the Human Body* by George Estreich was the winner of the 2003 contest, *Solar Prominence* by Kevin Craft was the 2004 winner, and *Gathering Sound* by Susan Davis and *Friday and the Year that Followed* by Juan J. Morales were the 2005 co-winners.

In addition to publishing the contest winners, the press has published two poetry collections by poets on the contest shortlist: *Night Highway* by Barbara Koons, and *Red Kimono, Yellow Barn* by David Hassler.

In 2005, the press published a creative nonfiction memoir, *Woman in the Water: A Memoir of Growing Up in Hollywoodland*, by Dorinda Clifton.

It is our hope that all of our books express our commitment to quality in writing and publishing. Please visit www.bedbugpress.com for more information about our press.